Wisdom Publications

Student Name: الإسم:

Student Address: العنوان:

School Name: إسم المدرسة:

Class: القسم:

Form/Year: السنة:

Teacher: المعلم:

Date Started: تاريخ البداية:

Date Completed: تاريخ النهاية:

SIMPLE STEPS IN QUR'AAN READING (PART 2)
A 3 PART SERIES

FIRST EDITION	1423	2003
SECOND EDITION	1429	2008

PREPARED BY
Abu-Saalihah Bin Ayyub
Zeenat-Ul-Qur'aan Academy
Nuneaton, England, UK

ISBN: 978-1-84828-077-9

PUBLISHED BY

Wisdom
Publications

© WISDOM PUBLICATIONS
Zeenat-Ul-Qur'aan Academy
PO Box 3157, Nuneaton
Warwickshire, CV11 5ZR
England - U.K.
info@wisdompublications.co.uk
www.wisdompublications.co.uk

Distributed by Azhar Academy Ltd.
54-68 Little Ilford Lane
Manor Park
London
E12 5QA
sales@azharacademy.com
www.azharacademy.com
TEL: +44 (020) 8911 9797
FAX: +44 (020) 8911 8999

DESIGN & PAGE SETTING:
Aslam Lorgat - Zi-Clone Multimedia UK
Ayyub Abbasi - SaiCom Graphic Designing INDIA
Abu-Saalihah Ayyub - UK

PREFACE

بسم الله الرحمن الرحيم

الحمدلله الذي علم الإنسان مالم يعلم . والصلوة والسلام على حبيبه محمد ﷺ إما بعد ....

All praises belong to our Creator and Sustainer Allah ﷻ and peace and blessings be upon our Beloved Nabi ﷺ , Aameen.

Dear Reader, by the grace of Allah you have in your hands the second complete edition of 'Simple Steps in Qur'aan Reading'. As the name suggests only a few simple steps are required in order to correctly recite and pronounce the Arabic alphabet letters directly from the Qur'aan.

We have made some amendments to this edition after receiving valuable advice from those scholars, teachers and parents who've used the previous edition and we hope you find these helpful.

Here are some of the changes we've made:

✓ *Arabic words taken directly from the Qur'aan - references are available on request; except Part One (initial lessons).*
✓ *Use of 'Majidi fonts' resembling the Majidi script. The preferential script of Qur'aans from the subcontinent.*
✓ *Use of Professional designers for the overall outlay and design.*
✓ *Adoption of colour coding for ease of understanding and recitation.*
✓ *Addition of simple colour coding from Surah Al-Fajr to An-Naas to aid in remembering rules of Tajweed.*

The Audio CD's have also been revamped:

✓ *The addition of an Explanatory note at the beginning of each lesson*
✓ *Recitation of the Arabic text by Shaykh Abu-Muhammad-Jibreel*
✓ *Narration of English text by a Year 2 Student*
✓ *Professional recording of CDs in Digital format*
✓ *Laminated and brightly coloured flash cards*
✓ *Qur'aan recitation CDs with individual tracks which correspond to individual lessons*
✓ *Colouring and writing books for young students*
✓ *A self study manual for Adults and older students*

This edition comes with an interactive CD to help students gain a better understanding. Additional support is available via our website.

Although we have taken the utmost care in the compilation and production of this book should you find any errors please don't hesitate in informing us. Your feedback is always welcome.

May Allah ﷻ forgive my shortcomings and accept this work as a means of acquiring his pleasure and closeness to his beloved Mustafa ﷺ.
May he reward my family, friends and well-wishers who've supported and encouraged me in continuing this noble work.

والله ولي التوفيق . نسأل الله أن ينفع به عموم المسلمين

Abu-Saalihah bin Ayyub
Khaadim-Ul-Qur'aan
Nuneaton, England
Muharram 10, 1428 AH

IN THE NAME OF ALLAH
MOST GRACIOUS, MOST MERCIFUL

FATHATAIN

FATHATAIN are Two Strokes (Two Fathahs)
above a letter. It sounds like the 'un' in B<u>un</u>. Fathatain
occurs only at the end of a word and always has an
Alif after it.

بِسْمِ اللهِ الرَّحْمٰنِ الرَّحِيْمِ

Lesson 1

Arabic Alphabet with Fathatain

جَّ	ثَّ	تَّ	بَّ	اَّ
رَّ	ذَّ	دَّ	خَّ	حَّ
ضَّ	صَّ	شَّ	سَّ	زَّ
فَّ	غَّ	عَّ	ظَّ	طَّ
نَّ	مَّ	لَّ	كَّ	قَّ
يَّ	ءَّ	هَّ	وَّ	

Simple Steps in Qur'aan reading

Comments:

Date Completed: /   /

Excellent ☐   Good ☐   Average ☐

Words with Fathatain

Lesson 2

طَبَقًا	رَغَدًا	اَبَدًا
مَثَلًا	مَلِكًا	جَنَفًا
لَعِبًا	قَصَصًا	عِنَبًا
قَدَرًا	اَسِفًا	ثَمَنًا
شَطَطًا	كَذِبًا	لَبَنًا
سُرُرًا	لُبَدًا	كُفُوًا

Comments:

Date Completed: / /

Excellent ☐ Good ☐ Average ☐

KASRATAIN

KASRATAIN are Two Strokes (Two Kasrahs) below a letter. It sounds like the 'in' in B<u>in</u>. Kasratain occurs only at the end of a word.

Arabic Alphabet with Kasratain

Lesson 3 _____

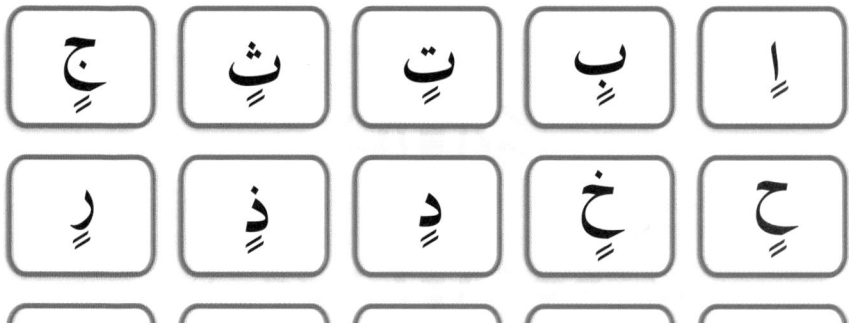

جٍ	ثٍ	تٍ	بٍ	اٍ
رٍ	ذٍ	دٍ	خٍ	حٍ
ضٍ	صٍ	شٍ	سٍ	زٍ
فٍ	غٍ	عٍ	ظٍ	طٍ
نٍ	مٍ	لٍ	كٍ	قٍ
يٍ	ءٍ	هٍ	وٍ	

Comments: Date Completed: /   /

Excellent ☐   Good ☐   Average ☐

Words with Kasratain

Lesson 4

كَبِدٍ	طَبَقٍ	عَمَدٍ
لَهَبٍ	مَسَدٍ	عَلَقٍ
شَجَرٍ	نَهَرٍ	بَلَدٍ
كَذَبٍ	سَحَرٍ	غَضَبٍ
بِدَمٍ	خَبَرٍ	فُرُشٍ
قَبَسٍ	اُكُلٍ	حَرَجٍ

Simple Steps in Qur'aan reading

Comments:

Date Completed: / /

Excellent ☐ Good ☐ Average ☐

DHAMMATAIN

DHAMMATAIN are two inverted commas
(Two Dhammahs) above a letter.
It sounds as the "un" in Running.
Dhammatain occurs only at the end of a word.

Lesson 5

Arabic Alphabet with Dhammatain

Simple Steps in Qur'aan reading

Comments:

Date Completed: / /

Excellent ☐ Good ☐ Average ☐

Words with Dhammatain

Lesson 6

كُتُبٌ	اُذُنٌ	سُرُرٌ
جُدَدٌ	رَجُلٌ	رُسُلٌ
بَشَرٌ	قَسَمٌ	اَحَدٌ
حَرَجٌ	مَرَضٌ	غُرَفٌ
وَلَدٌ	حُرُمٌ	لَعِبٌ
عَسِرٌ	ظُلَلٌ	اَشِرٌ

Comments:

Date Completed: /   /

Excellent ☐   Good ☐   Average ☐

Simple Steps In Qur'aan reading

SUKOON

SUKOON is also known as **JAZM.**
A Sukoon is like a small crescent appearing on top of
a letter. It is used to join letters.

Fathah with Sukoon

Lesson 7 _____

اً = اَنُ	بَّ = بَنُ	تًّ = تَنُ
ثًّ = ثَنُ	جًّ = جَنُ	حًّ = حَنُ
خًّ = خَنُ	دًّ = دَنُ	ذًّ = ذَنُ
رًّ = رَنُ	زًّ = زَنُ	سًّ = سَنُ
شًّ = شَنُ	صًّ = صَنُ	ضًّ = ضَنُ
طًّ = طَنُ	ظًّ = ظَنُ	عًّ = عَنُ

Comments:

Date Completed: /   /

Excellent ☐   Good ☐   Average ☐

Fathah with Sukoon

Lesson 8 _____

غُ = غَنُ	فُ = فَنُ	قُ = قَنُ
كُ = كَنُ	لُ = لَنُ	مُ = مَنُ
نُ = نَنُ	وُ = وَنُ	هُ = هَنُ
ءُ = ئَنُ		يُ = يَنُ

Comments: _____   Date Completed: /   /

Excellent ☐   Good ☐   Average ☐

بِسْمِ اللهِ الرَّحْمٰنِ الرَّحِيْمِ

Lesson 9

تٍ = تِنُ	بٍ = بِنُ	اٍ = اِنُ
حٍ = حِنُ	جٍ = جِنُ	ثٍ = ثِنُ
ذٍ = ذِنُ	دٍ = دِنُ	خٍ = خِنُ
سٍ = سِنُ	زٍ = زِنُ	رٍ = رِنُ
ضٍ = ضِنُ	صٍ = صِنُ	شٍ = شِنُ
عٍ = عِنُ	ظٍ = ظِنُ	طٍ = طِنُ

Comments: _____   Date Completed: /   /

Excellent ☐   Good ☐   Average ☐

Kasrah with Sukoon

Lesson 10 ___

قِنُ = قِ	فِنُ = فِ	غِنُ = غِ
مِنُ = مِ	لِنُ = لِ	كِنُ = كِ
هِنُ = هِ	وِنُ = وِ	نِنُ = نِ
يِنُ = يِ		ئِنُ = ءِ

Comments:

Date Completed: /   /

Excellent ☐   Good ☐   Average ☐

Lesson 11

Dhammah with Sukoon

اُنْ = اُ	بُنْ = بُ	تُنْ = تُ
ثُنْ = ثُ	جُنْ = جُ	حُنْ = حُ
خُنْ = خُ	دُنْ = دُ	ذُنْ = ذُ
رُنْ = رُ	زُنْ = زُ	سُنْ = سُ
شُنْ = شُ	صُنْ = صُ	ضُنْ = ضُ
طُنْ = طُ	ظُنْ = ظُ	عُنْ = عُ

Comments:

Date Completed: /   /

Excellent ☐   Good ☐   Average ☐

Lesson 12

Dhammah with Sukoon

غُنْ = غْ	فُنْ = فْ	قُنْ = قْ
كُنْ = كْ	لُنْ = لْ	مُنْ = مْ
نُنْ = نْ	وُنْ = وْ	هُنْ = هْ
ئُنْ = ءْ		يُنْ = يْ

Simple Steps in Qur'aan reading

Wisdom Publications

Separate and Joint Words

Lesson 13 _____

كُمْ	كُمُ	خَلُ	خَ لَ
وَعُ	وَعَ	لَقُ	لَ قَ
قُلُ	قُ لِ	اِذُ	اِذِ
اَطُ	اَطَ	عِلُ	عِ لَ
ثَرُ	ثَ رَ	زَعُ	زَ عَ
صَرُ	صَ رَ	بَلُ	بَ لَ

Comments:

Date Completed: /   /

Excellent ☐   Good ☐   Average ☐

Lesson 14

سَبْ	اَنْ	هُمْ	عَبْ	اَشْ
هَبْ	بَلْ	اِكْ	حَمْ	وَلْ
يَحْ	هَلْ	مُلْ	كَمْ	وَحْ
قُلْ	ذُقْ	عَنْ	اَمْ	اِنْ
لَمْ	اُشْ	مِنْ	اِذْ	قَدْ
قُلْ	يَشْ	حُضْ	اَطْ	مَغْ

Comments:

Date Completed: / /

Excellent ☐　　Good ☐　　Average ☐

Joining Partial Letters

Lesson 15

بِكُ	مُصُ	نَحُ	اَبُ
زِقُ	رَحُ	جَبُ	تُفُ
خَشُ	يَشُ	يُحُ	شِئُ
بَرُ	سَتُ	عِجُ	هِمُ
تَنُ	بِحُ	كِنُ	يَصُ
مُسُ	مَغُ	مُهُ	عَلُ

Comments:

Date Completed: / /

Excellent ☐   Good ☐   Average ☐

Joining 4 Letter Words

Lesson 16 _____

اَرْسَلَ	اَنْتُمْ	اَعْبُدُ	اَطْعَمَ
قَبْلِكَ	اُنْزِلَ	نَعْبُدُ	يَجْعَلُ
يَضْرِبُ	اَظْلَمَ	يَخْطَفُ	عَنْكُمْ
يُقْبَلُ	بِبَعْضٍ	نَصْبِرَ	يُفْسِدُ
بِعَهْدِ	اَعْلَمُ	مَعَكُمْ	وَلَهُمْ
كَذِكْرِ	اَقْرَرْ	شِئْتُمْ	مِنْكُمْ

Comments:

Date Completed: / /

Excellent ☐ Good ☐ Average ☐

Lesson 17

Joining 5 & 6 Letter Words

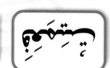

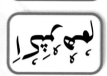

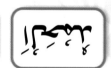
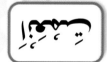
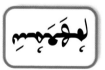

Simple Steps in Qur'aan reading

خطوة للقراءة الصحيحة للقرآن الكريم

YAA LEEN

WAAW LEEN

LETTERS OF LEEN

WAAW LEEN

بَوْ

If a **FATHAH** appears before **WAAW SAAKIN,** It will be known as **WAAW LEEN.** It is pronounced like the 'oe' sound in the word 'toe' and will be read quickly and swiftly.

Waaw Leen

Lesson 18 _____

جَوُ	ثَوُ	تَوُ	بَوُ	اَوُ
رَوُ	ذَوُ	دَوُ	خَوُ	حَوُ
ضَوُ	صَوُ	شَوُ	سَوُ	زَوُ
فَوُ	غَوُ	عَوُ	ظَوُ	طَوُ
نَوُ	مَوُ	لَوُ	كَوُ	قَوُ
يَوُ	ئَوُ	هَوُ	وَوُ	

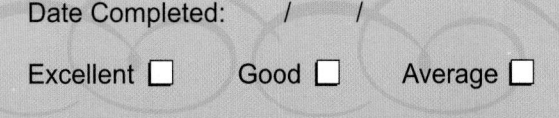

Comments:

Date Completed: /   /

Excellent ☐   Good ☐   Average ☐

Words with Waaw Leen

Lesson 19 _____

قَوۡمًا	سَوۡءٍ	يَوۡمَ
سَوۡفَ	خَوۡفٍ	صَوۡمَ
تَعۡثَوۡ	حَوۡلَ	اَوۡفِ
شَرَوۡهُ	اَوۡجَسَ	كَوۡثَرَ
يَوۡمَئِذٍ	وَمَوۡعِظَ	فِرۡعَوۡنَ
وَتَنۡسَوۡنَ	تُجۡزَوۡنَ	وَزَوۡجُكَ

Comments: Date Completed: /   /

Excellent ☐   Good ☐   Average ☐

YAA LEEN

If a **FATHAH** appears before **YAA SAAKIN,** It will be known as **YAA LEEN.** It is pronounced like the 'ai' sound in the word 'straight' and will be read quickly and swiftly.

Yaa Leen

Lesson 20

جَيْ	ثَيْ	تَيْ	بَيْ	اَيْ
رَيْ	ذَيْ	دَيْ	خَيْ	حَيْ
ضَيْ	صَيْ	شَيْ	سَيْ	زَيْ
فَيْ	غَيْ	عَيْ	ظَيْ	طَيْ
نَيْ	مَيْ	لَيْ	كَيْ	قَيْ
يَيْ	ئَيْ	هَيْ		وَيْ

Comments:

Date Completed: /   /

Excellent ☐   Good ☐   Average ☐

بِسْمِ اللهِ الرَّحْمٰنِ الرَّحِيْمِ

Words with Yaa Leen

Lesson 21

غَيْب	بَيْنَ	اَيْنَ
شَيْئًا	طَيْرًا	عَيْنٍ
يَدَيْهِ	بِغَيْرِ	صَيْفَ
اِلَيْهِمْ	بَيْنَهُمْ	اَبَوَيْهِ
اَوْحَيْتَ	عَيْنَيْنِ	فَاِلَيْنَا
فَأَنْجَيْنَ	كَيْدَهُمْ	عَلَيْهِمْ

Simple Steps In Qur'aan reading

Comments:

Date Completed: /   /

Excellent ☐   Good ☐   Average ☐

HUROOF-UL-MADD

The Three letters of Madd are:

 ALIF preceded by FATHAH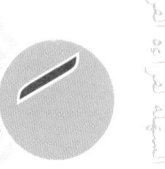

 WAAW preceded by DHAMMAH

 YAA preceded by KASRAH

ALIF MADDAH

بٰ / بَا

If the letter **ALIF** is after a **FATHAH**,
the **ALIF** will be stretched and
pronounced like 'a' in the word F<u>a</u>ther.
An **ERECT FATHAH** is also pronounced
like **ALIF MADDAH**

Alif Maddah

Lesson 22

بْ	بَا	اْ	اَا
ثْ	ثَا	تْ	تَا
حْ	حَا	جْ	جَا
دْ	دَا	خْ	خَا
رُ	رَا	ذْ	ذَا
سْ	سَا	زُ	زَا

Comments:

Date Completed: /   /

Excellent ☐   Good ☐   Average ☐

Alif Maddah

Lesson 23

شَا	شْ	صَا	صْ
ضَا	ضْ	طَا	طْ
ظَا	ظْ	عَا	عْ
غَا	غْ	فَا	فْ
قَا	قُ	كَا	كُ
لاَ	لْ	مَا	مُ

Comments:

Date Completed: / /

Excellent ☐   Good ☐   Average ☐

بِسْمِ اللهِ الرَّحْمٰنِ الرَّحِيْمِ

Alif Maddah

Lesson 24

وُ	وَا	نْ	نَا
ءُ	ءَا	هْ	هَا
يْ		يَا	

Simple Steps In Qur'aan reading

Comments:

Date Completed: / /

Excellent ☐   Good ☐   Average ☐

Words with Alif Maddah

Lesson 25

خَافَ	زَادَ	تَابَ
جُنَاحٌ	فَرَاغَ	قَالَ
خَادِعَ	جَاهَدَ	شَارِبَ
تَعَالَ	حَاسَبَ	قَاتِلَ
شَيْطَانٌ	اَنْدَادًا	كِتَابٌ
بِحِجَابٍ	طُغْيَانٍ	طَعَامٌ

Simple Steps In Qur'aan reading

Comments:

Date Completed: /   /

Excellent ☐   Good ☐   Average ☐

Words with Alif Maddah

Lesson 26

اٰدَمَ	اٰمَنَ	اِلٰهِ
اَبَوٰهُ	كِتٰبِ	ذٰلِكَ
فَذٰلِكَ	رَحْمٰنِ	مٰلِكِ
صٰلِحٰتِ	حٰفِظْتُ	قٰنِتَتُ
بِاَصْحٰبِ	ظُلِمْتُ	سَمٰوٰتِ
اَعْطَيْنٰكَ	رَزَقْنٰهُمْ	اَلٰهُكُمْ

Simple Steps In Qur'aan reading

Comments:

Date Completed: / /

Excellent ☐   Good ☐   Average ☐

WAAW MADDAH

If the letter **WAAW** is after a **DHAMMAH**, the **WAAW** will be stretched and pronounced like 'oo' as in the word Food. An **ERECT DHAMMAH** is also pronounced like <u>WAAW MADDAH</u>

Waaw Maddah

Lesson 27 ____

بٌ	بُوْ	أ	اُوْ
ثٌ	ثُوْ	ت	تُوْ
حْ	حُوْ	جْ	جُوْ
دْ	دُوْ	خْ	خُوْ
ئُ	رُوْ	ذْ	ذُوْ
ئَ	سُوْ	ژْ	زُوْ

Comments: Date Completed: /   /

Excellent ☐   Good ☐   Average ☐

Waaw Maddah

Lesson 28 _____

صُّ	صُوُ	شُ	شُوُ
طُ	طُوُ	ضُ	ضُوُ
عُ	عُوُ	ظُ	ظُوُ
فُ	فُوُ	غُ	غُوُ
كُ	كُوُ	قُ	قُوُ
مُ	مُوُ	ئُ	لُوُ

Comments:

Date Completed: /   /

Excellent ☐   Good ☐   Average ☐

Waaw Maddah

Lesson 29 _____

وُ	وُوُ	نْ	نُوُ
ءُ	ءُوُ	هْ	هُوُ
ئِي			يُوُ

Comments: Date Completed: /   /

Excellent ☐   Good ☐   Average ☐

بِسْمِ اللهِ الرَّحْمَنِ الرَّحِيمِ

Words with Waaw Maddah

Lesson 30

يُوْحَا	نُوْرُ	نُوْحُ
حُوْرٌ	طُوْرُ	أُوْتِيَ
وُجُوْهٌ	تَكُوْنُ	بُوْرِكَ
قَارُوْنُ	هَارُوْنَ	هَارُوْتَ
أُوْتُوْهُ	سَبَقُوْنَا	عٰكِفُوْنَ
دَاخِرُوْنَ	رُءُوْسَكُمْ	مُسْلِمُوْنَ

Simple Steps In Qur'aan reading

Comments:

Date Completed: /   /

Excellent ☐   Good ☐   Average ☐

Words with Waaw Maddah

Lesson 31 _____

لَهٗ	مَالَهٗ	اٰيَاتَهٗ
حَوْلَهٗ	نَبَذَهٗ	فِئَتُهٗ
اَجْرَهٗ	دَاوٗدَ	وَجْهَهٗ
وَوُرِىَ	جُنُوْدُهٗ	سُبْحٰنَهٗ
رَحْمَتُهٗ	رَسُوْلَهٗ	مَوْءٗدَةُ
تِلَاوَتَهٗ	يَسْتَوٗنَ	يَعْرِفُوْنَهٗ

Comments:

Date Completed: / /

Excellent ☐   Good ☐   Average ☐

YAA MADDAH

If the letter **YAA** is after a **KASRAH,**
the **YAA** will be stretched and
pronounced like 'ee' as in the word F<u>ee</u>d.
An **ERECT KASRAH** is also pronounced
like YAA MADDAH

Lesson 32

ب	بِي	ا	اِي
ث	ثِي	ت	تِي
ح	حِي	ج	جِي
د	دِي	خ	خِي
ر	رِي	ذ	ذِي
س	سِي	ز	زِي

Simple Steps In Qur'aan reading

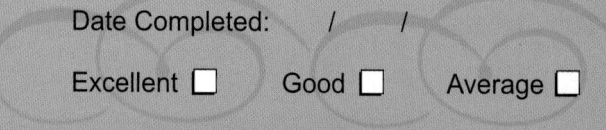

Comments:

Date Completed: /   /

Excellent ☐   Good ☐   Average ☐

Lesson 33

صِ	صِي	شِ	شِي
طِ	طِي	ضِ	ضِي
عِ	عِي	ظِ	ظِي
فِ	فِي	غِ	غِي
كِ	كِي	قِ	قِي
مِ	مِي	لِ	لِي

Comments: Date Completed: / /

Excellent ☐   Good ☐   Average ☐

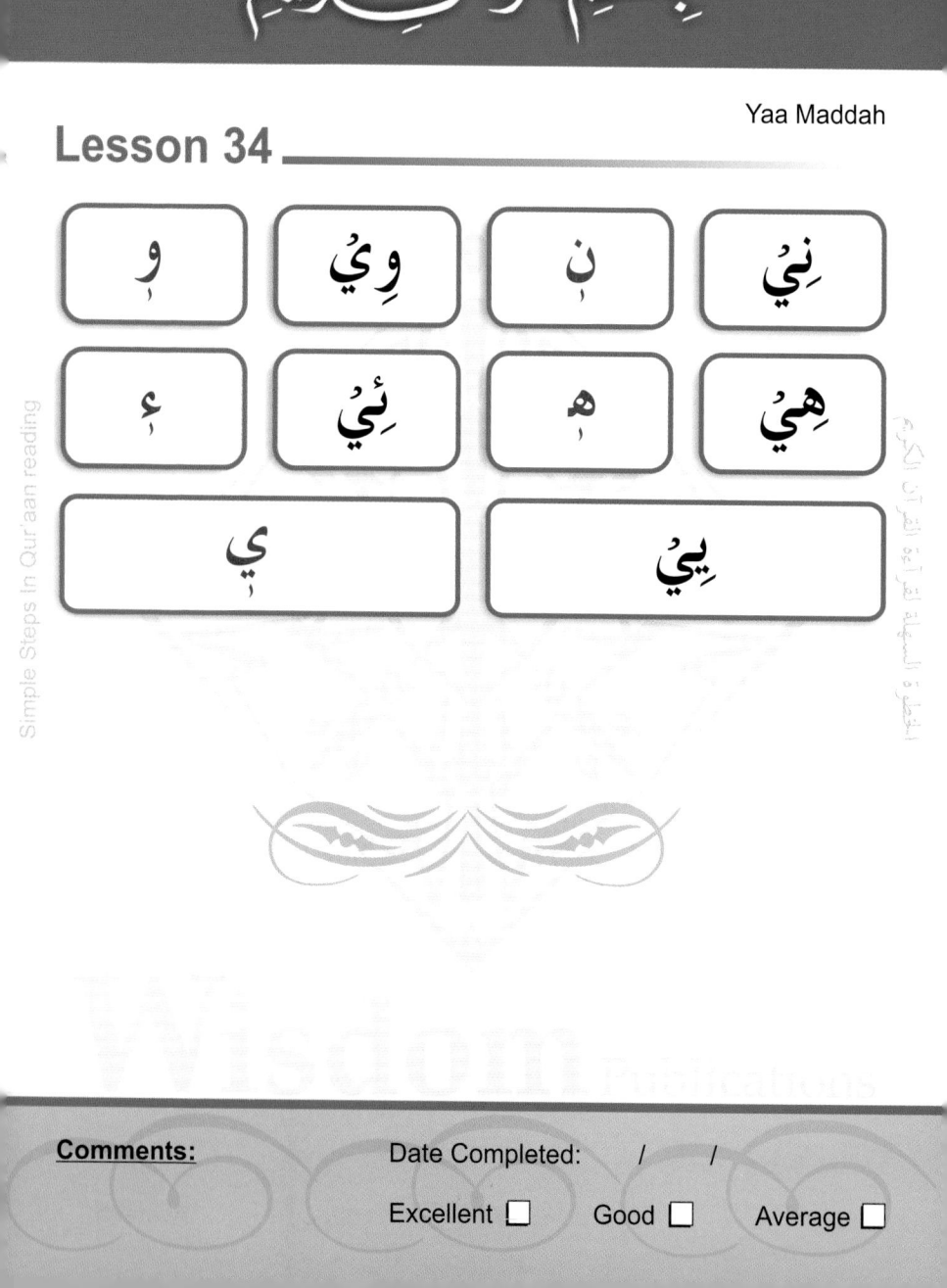

بِسْمِ اللهِ الرَّحْمٰنِ الرَّحِيْمِ

Yaa Maddah

Lesson 34

نِيْ	نْ	وِيُ	وِ
هِيْ	هْ	ئِيُ	ءْ

| يِيْ | | يْ | |

Simple Steps In Qur'aan reading

Comments:

Date Completed: /   /

Excellent ☐   Good ☐   Average ☐

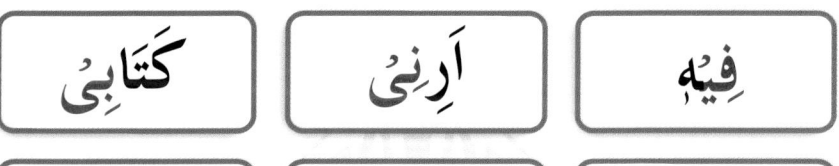

Lesson 35 _____

كِتَابِى	اَرِنِى	فِيهِ
دِينِى	اُجِيبُ	مَقَادِيرَ
رَازِقِينَ	لَذِينَ	عِبَادِى
مُهِينٌ	يُوَارِى	عَذَابِى
مُحِيطٌ	حَكِيمٌ	عَظِيمٌ
تَمَاثِيلَ	تَضْلِيلٍ	مَفَاتِيحُ

Simple Steps In Qur'aan reading

Comments:

Date Completed: / /

Excellent ☐ Good ☐ Average ☐

Words with Yaa Maddah

Lesson 36

الْفِ	اُحْيِ	بِهِ
مِثْلِهِ	اٰيٰتِهِ	عِبَادِهِ
وَرُسُلِهِ	رَاْسِهِ	بَعْدِهِ
بِاَمْرِهِ	وَقِيْلِهِ	مِيْثَاقِهِ
وَزَوْجِهِ	تِلَاوَتِهِ	الْفِهِمُ
بِمُزَحْزِحِهِ	بِرَحْمَتِهِ	يَسْتَحْيِ

Comments:

Date Completed: / /

Excellent ☐   Good ☐   Average ☐

Lesson 37

قَّ	قَا	قُ	قَ
ضٍ	ضِي	ضٍ	ضٍ
ظُّ	ظُو	ظْ	ظُ
غً	غَا	غْ	غَ
رُّ	رُو	ءَ	رُ
لٍ	لِي	لْ	لِ

Simple Steps In Qur'aan reading

Comments:

Date Completed: / /

Excellent ☐ Good ☐ Average ☐

بِسْمِ اللّٰهِ الرَّحْمٰنِ الرَّحِيْمِ

Mixed Symbols

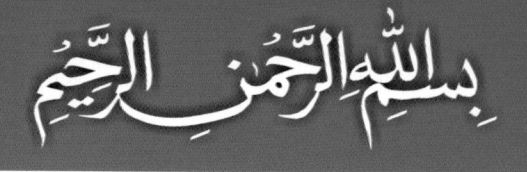

Lesson 38

صْ	كً	شِ	قَ
طِ	يِ	ضْ	ضِيْ
لْ	صٍ	مِيْ	ظِيْ
طِيْ	عُوْ	شِيْ	غٌ
كْ	نَا	اُوْ	قِيْ
مْ	رَا	طُوْ	لِ

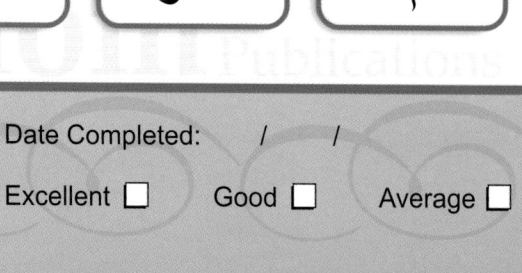

Comments:

Date Completed: / /

Excellent ☐ Good ☐ Average ☐

Lesson 39

مِنْ غَيْرِهِ

كُفُوًا اَحَدُۢ

لِمَنْ خَشِيَ

وَاسِعٌ اَلِيْمٌ

طَيْرًا اَبَابِيْلَ

مِنْهُ خِطَابًا

شَاكِرٌ عَلِيْمٌ

يَوْمَئِذٍ عَلَيْهَا

كِتَابٌ حَكِيْمٌ

عَذَابٌ غَلِيْظٌ

حَاسِدٍ اِذَا حَسَدَ

كِرَامًا كَاتِبِيْنَ

Comments:

Date Completed: ___ / ___ / ___

Excellent ☐   Good ☐   Average ☐

Lesson 40

فَاِذَا دَفَعْتُمْ اِلَيْهِمْ اَمْوَالَهُمْ

وَلَاجُنَاحَ عَلَيْكُمْ فِيْمَا تَرَاضَيْتُمْ

عَقَدَتْ اَيْمَانُكُمْ فَاٰتُوْهُمْ نَصِيْبَهُمْ

اَوْ اَعْرِضْ عَنْهُمْ وَاِنْ تُعْرِضْ عَنْهُمْ

كَانَتَا تَحْتَ عَبْدَيْنِ مِنْ عِبَادِنَا

صَالِحَيْنِ فَخَانَتٰهُمَا فَلَمْ يُغْنِيَا عَنْهُمَا

Comments:

Date Completed: / /

Excellent ☐   Good ☐   Average ☐

قالوا سبحانك لا علم لنا إلا ما علمتنا إنك أنت العليم الحكيم

"**Glory be** to you, we have no knowledge except what you have taught us.
Verily, it is You, the All Knower, the All Wise,".
Surah Al-Baqarah-32

Ma-Sha'-Allah!
Congratulation
On Completing

"Simple Steps in Qur'aan Reading – Part 2"

You may now commence
Part 3 of the series

We pray that you will find Part 3
As enjoyable too .... Aameen !

Affiliated to:
Zeenat-Ul-Qur'aan Academy

PUBLISHED BY:

Wisdom
Publications

WISDOM PUBLICATIONS
info@wisdompublications.co.uk
www.wisdompublications.co.uk

FIRST EDITION	1423	2003	الطبعة الأولى
SECOND EDITION	1429	2008	الطبعة الثانية

الطبعة الأولى ١٤٢٣ ه‍ ٢٠٠٣م
الطبعة الثانية ١٤٢٩ ه‍ ٢٠٠٨م